Diving

BY S.L. HAMILTON

WILD WATER

A&D Xtreme
An imprint of Abdo Publishing | www.abdopublishing.com

Visit us at
www.abdopublishing.com

Published by Abdo Publishing Company, a division of ABDO, PO Box 398166, Minneapolis, Minnesota 55439. Copyright ©2016 by Abdo Consulting Group, Inc. International copyrights reserved in all countries. No part of this book may be reproduced in any form without written permission from the publisher. A&D Xtreme™ is a trademark and logo of Abdo Publishing Company.

Printed in the United States of America, North Mankato, Minnesota.
052015
092015

 PRINTED ON RECYCLED PAPER

Editor: John Hamilton
Graphic Design: Sue Hamilton
Cover Design: Sue Hamilton
Cover Photo: Getty Images
Interior Photos: Alamy-pgs 18-19 & 20-21, AP-pgs 8-9, 9 (inset), 10, 11, 12-13, 14-15, 26-27, 28, 29 & 30-31; Casa Bonita Mexican Restaurant-pgs 22-23; Corbis-pg 4-5, Getty Images-pgs 16-17, 24 & 25; iStock-pgs 1, 2-3, 30-31 (diving silhouettes) & 32; Missouri History Museum-St. Louis-pgs 6-7.

Websites
To learn more about Wild Water action, visit booklinks.abdopublishing.com. These links are routinely monitored and updated to provide the most current information available.

Library of Congress Control Number: 2015930947

Cataloging-in-Publication Data

Hamilton, S.L.
  Diving / S.L. Hamilton.
    p. cm. -- (Wild water)
  ISBN 978-1-62403-750-4
  1. Diving--Juvenile literature.   I. Title.
  797--dc23
                                          2015930947

Contents

Diving

Diving is the skill of jumping from a fixed platform or a flexible springboard. A dive can be a simple hands-over-the-head entry into the water. Or it can include acrobatic movements such as somersaults or twists. Divers try to enter the water perfectly vertical, making as little splash as possible.

Divers train to make their dives perfect. The sport requires precise timing and controlled body movements. A diver cannot be afraid of heights. Diving can be beautiful or it can be deadly.

XTREME QUOTE – "A diver is one part acrobat, two parts test pilot." –Unknown

History

Diving likely began with early people having fun by jumping into the water. In the 1700s, amazing dives from rocks and cliffs were made by natives from Acapulco, Mexico, and Lanai, Hawaii. A plain dive known as a "plunge" became popular in Great Britain in the late 1800s. Athletes dove, or "plunged," into the water, gliding face down as far as they could for 60 seconds.

"Fancy diving" began with gymnasts in Sweden and Germany. These athletes practiced their moves in the water to prevent injury. Their acrobatic twists and somersaults were beautiful to watch. By the early 1900s, diving was a sport of its own.

Frank Kehoe of the United States diving at the 1904 Summer Olympic Games.

XTREME FACT – *Diving as an Olympic sport first took place at the 1904 Summer Olympic Games in St. Louis, Missouri. There were two events: platform diving and plunge for distance. Both events were won by the United States.*

Platform Diving

Platform divers perform amazing acrobatic moves from a rigid tower or platform into a pool. The platforms are usually 5 meters (16 feet), 7.5 meters (25 feet), or 10 meters (33 feet) tall. Divers can take off from their dives either facing forward or backward. They may also do an armstand dive, beginning from a handstand.

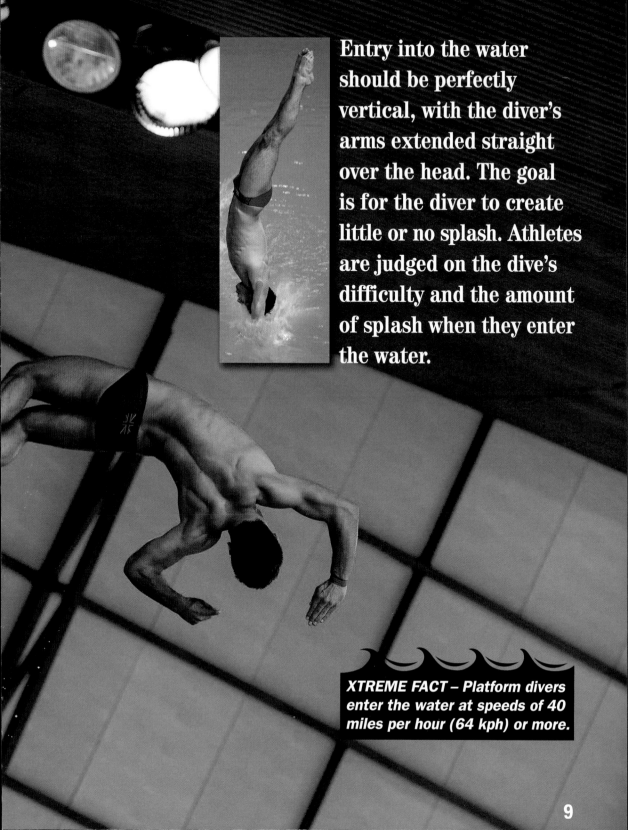

Entry into the water should be perfectly vertical, with the diver's arms extended straight over the head. The goal is for the diver to create little or no splash. Athletes are judged on the dive's difficulty and the amount of splash when they enter the water.

XTREME FACT – Platform divers enter the water at speeds of 40 miles per hour (64 kph) or more.

Springboard Diving

Springboard divers use a flexible diving board to add height to their takeoff. The extra height allows divers to perform more complex acrobatic moves. Dives are divided into six groups: forward, backward, reverse, inward, twisting, and armstand. In competition, divers must perform dives from each of the groups, except the armstand. Armstands are never performed from the springboard.

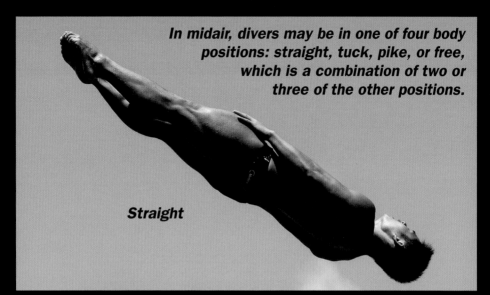

In midair, divers may be in one of four body positions: straight, tuck, pike, or free, which is a combination of two or three of the other positions.

Straight

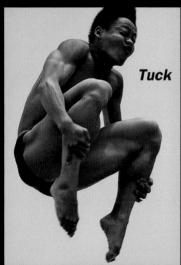

Tuck

Pike

Free (performing a twist)

Synchronized Diving

Synchronized diving is a sport where two divers mirror each other. The idea arose from synchronized swimming competitions. Synchro diving became an Olympic sport in 2000. It quickly became very popular.

Judges look for how closely the two divers are in sync. This includes the takeoff, height, acrobatic movements, and pool entry. Synchronized divers compete from a 10-meter (33-foot) -high platform or from a 3-meter (10-foot) -high springboard.

XTREME FACT – *Sometimes synchronized divers perform opposite each other. For example, one diver might execute a forward dive, while the other performs a reverse dive. This is known as a pinwheel.*

Cliff Diving

Cliff diving requires extreme body control, courage, and concentration. Cliff divers jump from heights of 57 to 86 feet (17 to 26 m). They have about 3 seconds to perform their dive. They enter the water feet first, often going as fast as 50 mph (80 kph). Cold water landings are more painful than warm water. Saltwater landings are harder because saltwater is denser than freshwater.

XTREME FACT – Hitting the water head first on a cliff dive can kill a person.

15

Steven LoBue of the United States dives 89 feet (27 m) off a cliff face during the 2014 Red Bull Cliff Diving World Series in Azores, Portugal.

There are several cliff diving competitions. The World High Diving Federation was formed in 1996. It sponsors the International Cliff Diving Championship in Switzerland. The Red Bull Cliff Diving World Series travels to locations such as Bosnia, France, Italy, Mexico, Portugal, Spain, and Texas.

High Diving

High diving requires men to jump from a platform 89 feet (27 m) high. Women jump from a platform that is 66 feet (20 m) high. Athletes must perform acrobatic moves and then enter the water feet first during a dive. The body must be straight, feet together, and toes pointed.

XTREME FACT – No one under age 18 may compete in high diving because of the extreme danger. Divers hit the water at about 60 mph (97 kph). If they hit the water wrong, they can be knocked out or killed.

France's Cyrille Oumedjkane competes in the men's high diving final at the FINA World Championships in Barcelona, Spain, in 2013.

FINA (Federation Internationale de Natation) sponsors high diving competitions. This includes the World Aquatics Championships and the new High Diving World Cup. The first High Diving World Cup was held in Kazan, Russia, in 2014. During the flight (time to the water), divers may perform somersaults, pikes, tucks, or twists. The dive is finished when the diver is completely below the water's surface. For safety, rescue scuba divers are positioned in the water to assist every diver.

Indoor High Diving

Divers entertain diners at the Casa Bonita Mexican restaurant in Denver, Colorado. A 30-foot (9-m) -tall indoor waterfall stands over a deep pool inside the building. From a ledge, divers stand on realistic-looking cliffs and perform amazing high dives into the water below.

XTREME FACT – A "rip" is the perfect low-splash entry into the water by a diver. It is called a rip because of the sound made by the water entry.

Shallow Diving

Shallow diving requires an athlete to jump from a high height into a shallow pool of water. To accomplish this type of dive, athletes must hold their bodies horizontally. This is the opposite of all other diving. Some call this dive a "belly flop."

Darren Taylor, also known as Professor Splash, holds the world record in shallow diving. In 2011, he dove from 36 feet 3 inches (11.05 m) into just 11.8 inches (30 cm) of water. This is like diving off a three-story building. "The real big trick with this dive," Taylor says, "is to land flat. I try to get as much water out of the pool as I can. I want to dissipate as much water for a cushion effect."

XTREME QUOTE – "Yes, it hurts, but the pain lasts for a minute, while the glory lasts a lifetime!" —Darren Taylor, Professor Splash

Dangers

Divers train for years to perfect their sport. One of the greatest issues for many divers is the risk of hitting the platform or springboard. An arm or leg can be broken by the impact. If a diver's head hits, it can knock them out or even kill them.

American diver Greg Louganis hit his head at the Summer Olympic Games in Seoul, Korea, in 1988. He suffered a cut to his scalp, but went on to win gold medals in springboard and platform events.

In scoring a dive, judges will take off points for being dangerously close to the board. Normally, a diver should be within 2 feet (.6 m) of the platform.

XTREME FACT – In 1983, 21-year-old Sergei Chalibashvili hit his head on the diving platform. He was attempting to do a 3½ reverse somersault in tuck position. The Soviet diver died days later. His dive became known as the "dive of death."

Divers face many risks. Cliff divers must watch the waves and surf to be sure they dive when the water is deepest. All divers risk hitting their heads on the pool or sea bottom. To avoid injury, divers must enter the water vertically. (Only shallow divers enter the water horizontally.) Diving accidents include being knocked unconscious, paralysis, or even death.

United States diver Chelsea Davis hit her head on the springboard during the 2005 World Aquatics Championships in Montreal, Canada. Davis required stitches at a local hospital.

A teen dives off a 40-foot (12 m) rock cliff face at "The Deeps" in Duluth, Minnesota. The area has many jutting rock ledges. Divers must run and jump to avoid these rocks. Those who do not leap far enough have ended up with serious injuries, including broken bones and concussions.

Glossary

ACROBATIC MOVES
Movements that include tumbling and dancing. Acrobatic moves include such things as somersaults and twists.

ARMSTAND GROUP DIVES
Dives that begin with the athlete in a handstand position on a platform.

BACKWARD GROUP DIVES
Dives where the athlete stands at the end of the board with his or her back to the water. The diver jumps and rotates away from the board.

FORWARD GROUP DIVES
Dives where the athlete begins by facing forward, jumps, and rotates front toward the water.

FRESHWATER
Water sources with little amounts of salt in them, such as most lakes and rivers. Saltwater, such as water in oceans and seas, has a higher salt content.

Inward Group Dives
Dives where the athlete stands at the end of the board with his or her back to the water, jumps out, and rotates toward the board.

Reverse Group Dives
Dives where the athlete stands facing the water, jumps, and rotates toward the board.

Saltwater
Water with a heavier salt content than freshwater, about 35 parts per thousand. This is found in Earth's seas and oceans.

Synchronized
In diving, when two people move in the exact same way.

Tuck
When a diver bends at both the knees and the hips so that the body is in a ball-like shape.

Twisting Group Dives
Dives that use a twisting motion in midair. These can be forward, backward, reverse, or inward twists.

Unconscious
A person who is not awake or aware of what is going on around them.

Index